Tip it

Written by Zoë Clarke

Illustrated by Ley Honor Roberts

Collins

a tin pan

mat

tin

tap

3

a tin man

tip a tap

6

tip a map

tip a tin

tip a pan

mat

man

tin

tin

pan

pad

12

/t/

14

After reading

Letters and Sounds: Phase 2

Word count: 36

Focus phonemes: /a/ /t/ /p/ /i/ /n/ /m/ /d/

Curriculum links: Understanding the World: People and communities

Early learning goals: Listening and attention: listen to stories, accurately anticipating key events and respond to what is heard with relevant comments, questions or actions; Understanding: answer 'how' and 'why' questions about experiences and in response to stories or events; Reading: children use phonic knowledge to decode regular words and read them aloud accurately

Developing fluency

- Go back and read the chant to your child, using lots of expression.
- Make sure that your child follows as you read.
- Pause so that your child can join in and read with you.
- Say the whole chant together. You can make up some actions to go with the words.

a tin pan	tip a pan
a tin man	mat, man, tin
tip a tap	pad, map, pin
tip a map	tin, pan, pad
tip a tin	mat, map, tap

Phonic practice

- Say the word **tin**. Ask your child if they can sound out each of the letter sounds in the word, **tin** t/i/n. Now blend them. Do the same with the following words:

  tip   tap   pan   man

- Now look at the 'I spy sounds' on pages 14 and 15 together. Which words can your child find in the picture with the 't' sound in them? (e.g. *tap, teddy, train, tractor, tea, toast*)